For Dontá—

Under the Sky They Lit Cities

Thank you for everything! You made our stay in Portland...

Best,
Travis Cebula

4/29/2011

Under the Sky They Lit Cities

Travis Cebula

BlazeVOX [books]

Buffalo, New York

Under the Sky They Lit Cities by Travis Cebula
Copyright © 2010

Published by BlazeVOX [books]

All rights reserved. No part of this book may be reproduced without
the publisher's written permission, except for brief quotations in reviews.

Printed in the United States of America

Book design by Geoffrey Gatza

First Edition
ISBN: 978-1-60964-025-5
Library of Congress Control Number 2010931941

BlazeVOX [books]
303 Bedford Ave
Buffalo, NY 14216

Editor@blazevox.org

publisher of weird little books

BlazeVOX [books]

blazevox.org

2 4 6 8 0 9 7 5 3 1

B   X

Acknowledgements

The author wishes to acknowledge the following publications for sharing poems from this book with the world:

"Under the Sky They Lit Cities" in A *Trunk of Delirium*
Selections from "Agnostic" in *BlazeVOX* 2K9
Selections from "Agnostic" in *Flaneur Foundry 2, sleep prngrphr.*
"Graves in the Snow Near Krakow" in *(R)evolve*
"Invocation," "Memory of a Yardlight," and "Passing time Downtown" in *Whrrds*
"Sometimes the Sky in Golden" in *Monkey Puzzle*

I would also like to extend my gratitude to my wife, Anselm Hollo, Will Alexander, and especially Elizabeth Robinson—all of whom must receive credit for anything good this book has to offer. Geoffrey Gatza also deserves my eternal thanks for giving this manuscript a happy home.

Under the Sky They Lit Cities

Invocation 15

Suburbs are Fragments 17

Graves in the Snow near Krakow 19

Memory of a Yardlight 22

Sometimes, the Sky in Golden 26

Passing Time Downtown 27

Etude for Cities *(as seen by the sky)* 28

The Sky Shrinks As 41

Agnostic 43

Under the Sky They Lit Cities 92

Whiteout, Early Morning 93

Oh, the passenger
He rides and he rides
He sees things from under glass
He looks through his window's eye
He sees the things he knows are his
He sees the bright and hollow sky
He sees the city asleep at night
He sees the stars are out tonight
And all of it is yours and mine

                        -Iggy Pop, *The Passenger*

Under the Sky
They Lit Cities

For everyone who ever fell in love with a city.

Invocation

a raven flies
somewhere between
                farm and polis,
          grass or glass—

                        sometime between streetcars
                            viaducts crumbled—

          in the evening.
          black Morrigan
          surveys tumbled tracts

where hunch-backed gardeners

      nurtured
              a thin

corruption.

                        seductive City,
                        your eyes reflect
                            blue lights.
                    tell me a story of the boy
                      who kissed your neck,

              a story before your smile

        twisted.

Suburbs are Fragments

       mountains

to the city, to

     mundane

          struggle

 stay

 one thing

              lights of the blue

Graves in the Snow near Krakow

We know this much—that my great-grandmother boarded a ship for America [alone] in the early part of the 20th century.

[I know this because her steamer trunk stays in the corner storing blankets. My mother painted the latch brass to make it beautiful]

let's say it was 1908 because in truth there's no reason not to.

let's say also that her name was Ana and that she was short and slight of build.

[she held me tiny in the months before she died and I know this because her yellow quilt was always on the bed in the guestroom]

she was sixteen and migrating to The New World in that steamship moment where immigrant and emigrant penetrate and linger.

so many from Poland in that maze of rivets shared the salt chill and the smell of leather.

the dream of paper.

a rubber stamp.

We know too that she found her way onto a train and thus to St. Joseph Missouri with its stockyards and meat packing.

the blood and mud the stained wood .

rubber boots.

[I remember November in western Kansas on the family farm and Uncle Junior bringing long rings of kielbasa from St. Joseph and how they reeked of garlic—would be wrapped four layers deep in foil and butcher paper and still ruin a cooler]

story has it she met my great grandfather and my great grandfather both there.

let's say their names were Adam and Tom because we know no others. [Cebula and Bindyk]

It is clear that from Missouri my family [in its various components and luggage and children] rode the train to Edson Kansas.

from the depot they walked with everything they had to what would be the farm.

and the farm next to it the family farm too.

family history tells us that this is not the same farm my father grew up on.

not the same gable window in which I watched the sun rise over the hulk of a rusting combine.

my grandfather borrowed the money to drill a well on that ground and may have even been the first one to do it in the county they say.

I knew the farm was big because the pipes seemed to stretch for miles. [and because my grandfather would share his donut and coffee with me on the bench seat of his Ford in the time between one end of the cornfield and the other]

A few years ago my father's sister Janice went to Poland [as well as Assisi] on a pilgrimage and [we know she did this because she told us and showed the pictures]

Janice is Franciscan and took a side trip from Assisi to Poland. [our family's home]

We know Ana and the rest came from a small town outside of Krakow because that's what the rumors were.

let's call it Wieliczka because in truth there's no reason not to.

the people there told her that there used to be many Cebulas but they all went away.

and we also know that there were no written records of the family in Wieliczka.[we know this because we know churches always burn]

Janice told us that she found names on limestone grave markers in an old churchyard.

let's say that the names read something like Ana and Tom and Adam and Cebula and Bindyk and Nerka and the like because in truth there's no reason not to say it.

none at all.

and let's say that the dates on these graves all read 1908.

We know that my great-grandparents never talked about Poland.

because they didn't.

Memory of a Yardlight

on the farm there was
a mercury streetlamp attached—

      rusted bolts from a splintered city
      groped into
      rotting boards.

    second floor
of the milk house,
        as a child
              I never understood
                      two stories,
      no stairs,
and a windmill.
      no arms.

by that cool masonry room
my uncles boiled
        carcasses of pheasants
        in a trashbarrel overflowing.
              they plucked steaming feathers
                  onto November snow.

I know
what's there,
above the rusted stove—
    [I took pulls from the sneaked
        bottle of schnapps]
                water,
              pipes and light.
                light on the side.
              light for the yard.

the walls slump
into gentle collapse.

                        an attic
                        returns to ground.

I will sift the soft splinters
                                        and rake away
                            the room behind.

the blue light
wriggled its way into
the gravel yard
                    into its windbreak of dying elms

            buffalo grass

        plum bushes

and junebugs
                            even in July
                                        and on through August.

Somewhere Between Cities and Descent

        I rode home in cars
                tired, sad,
                  rolling the highway down
          from the mountains
                      to the city, to home.
                  mundane, brittle.

young

        eyes struggled
to stay awake,
            make it last—
        one thing for all special

  ones.

                lights of the blue city,
                Denver, spread wide
                      as clutching arms...

        every time

a little different,
a little dirtier, more orange.

                a little older.

A Plastic Sack of Clean Folded Linen

it used to be a Dodge Neon—

   compact, mint-green,   efficient.

   it used to be.

 somewhere
            a scrap yard cradles

its cube
of rust,
hints of chrome,
           and sheets rotting with the rain.

                                              there is so much safety
                                              glass, faceted squares
                                              everywhere, on the floor
                                              on the seat, on the sill.
                                              they cover the wailing baby,
                                                    fill his bucket.

    later   we return

to collect   our baggage,

  tugging.

but the poor   tortured   wreck

     has bitten down,   hard

and won't let go.

Sometimes, the Sky in Golden

a chill wind should be
the one to draw leaves from high cradles
in this clipped enclave
of comfort and knee-high fences.

whisper it's the season of the hard moon,
hung two fingers above the skyline.
wearily I watch the rock mesa rise to it.

some say harvest moon, which sounds
soft, but it cracks our pond—shatters
into our kitchen in the hours before dawn:
the only thing that ever made the dog growl.

whether out of rage, domesticity, or innocent fear
on this morning my exit makes wood ducks warble
as the door clacks shut behind me.

they are soft golden still, young round leaves,
and have not yet begun to snap
and scuttle until raked into black sacks.

somewhere beyond these yards and glistening spider webs, I see
the flat blue face finally sink as a single coyote howls.

Passing Time Downtown

my mother dropped me

    on the boulevard at lunch.

I disappeared

      into the city,

        sank in a river of black leather and wool.

          torsos flowed

ahead to the right,   back to the left.

    salesmen, bankers, drunks, whores.

        for a few hours

      I partook

    in walking.

    I feared loss

                    of momentum:

to sit down at a concrete table

                across from a transient

    only to lose again

        at chess.

Etude for Cities
(as seen by the sky)

1.

      it is truth:

                         theists entice unities.

           the skyline directs—
           encysts, kindles, entitles.

    it suckled the eyeless settler,
                hustled scenery in its tensile thunder.
the killers cheered.

2.

                                    in the
    silence
                                                      cruelty tinkles...
              stunted shyster,
                his tureens of shekels.

this is how the thinker litters.
this is how the student studies dryness.

3.

        streets.

hitters.

        deniers.

nudists.

        shticks.

shrinks.

        sleuths.

shrieks.

        shrines.

trinity.

4.

the recluse retched.
  his helices rustled thickly,
                        their density utterly chinked.
        the hirsute decline
         from endless insults—

  crudity thus ensured.

5.

        resilience.
incredulities indiscreetly silkscreened...
    credulities intersected...
              disinterest disinherits ethnicity:
  telekinetic,
                                     iridescent.

6.

        industries

    christened disunities,
   interested indirectly in resiliency:
                      the rickitiest turnstiles,
                      the kitchiest heuristics.

itchy lucidities.

  they huckster the slenderest to the thirstiest.
  their teensiest cruelness unsettles.

7.

    the strictest nihilists
   inherited necessity.

           their lucidness stretches,
          centuries unsettled,
       destitute interests,
their cruelties...
                      sincerely,
                  the scientist intercedes.
              he resettles light
                  in its stylistic litheness.

8.

the trinities and chiselers are sincerest,
the sturdiest and the sluttiest.
dirtiness rekindles their stuttered destinies:

    sterility,

            clustered derelicts,

    listeners.

triteness underlies luridness,

    lights
their stenciled utilities.

9.

      heredity reclines serenely,
                       thickset.
like the nihilist who reelects curtness.
          he lessens his listener.
                              cursedly centrist,

                    there is no sinecure.

10.

the city's likeness
rekindles ethylene,
enriches skylines.
the cruelest here resulted
from neuritis.

eternity!
shit!
insults!
the lyricist stutters.
senility is truly the reediest serenity.

it is a district of lucidity.
it is a district of security.
only the drunkest entities teetered.

11.

the identity of this resident is tuneless.
           here heresies ridicule suicides.

        the huntress intrudes—
                         sinister herd,
    her children shriek
                  settlers!
                  cultists!
                  residues!

12.

treeless silences—
                here the luckiest distrust.

      this city inherits
               disunity,
                      sureties,
                              rudeness,
                                      slickers.

13.

tenuity distils:

       redneck ,   inducer,   lyncher,   trustee.

       the lustre of sundered duchies.

The Sky Shrinks As

the sun slumps
into the mountains,
stubborn night refuses
to stoop.

                it is less
                that things light up,
                than that they just don't go dark;
                only fade to concentric
                rings of electricity:
                orange bound around glass carbuncles
                that relegate darkness
                to the wedges of space between.

in a city of light,
crowds multiply in aggregate.
an effect accentuated
by storm,
and—in particular—snow...
with attendant low clouds
and matte reflection.

                nighttime was once
                a paradigm of dark,
                now a paragon of pink,
                or puce.
                ghastly silhouettes—
                nominate dimness in absentia.
                drooling shadows
                stand in
                for objects, hapless
                in the path
                of streetlights.

this is our legacy,
staining the heavens
on the forked tail of radio static.
a glow rises,
infecting the twilight by increments:
not so much a planet
as a lack of space.

Agnostic

Urgently I burrowed in. The city.

   Not intending to condemn, I have
        demolished the beauty of boulevards—dust
   eclipses the gorgeous glimpse:

   revolving glass doors
        trimmed in brass.
      Hot steam rises from quiet streets.

            Eventually details overwhelm me.

Sarcasm ensues, goads me,

        knock flat any
           yearning for exuberance
        that I might have been nurturing.

        λ

Here's something to chew on—

        employment breeds contempt as surely as any

    yellow impulse in time of war.

Lurching blind and dead every morning.

    In a city no longer screened,

        tragic overcoats trail attachés.

            λ

Can I possibly ignore executives

    in favor of
        the few poppies

interred in concrete boxes? Periodic

        episodes of color dot grey
           sidewalks.

  In another city flowers flourish in rows, white or even blue.
    Nomadic gardeners clad in coveralls plant them.

      Three walk by; their clanking
          echoes off buildings as they drag hoes and Japanese
    reapers in hooked curves behind them. I swear they look
        just like men here, fixing potholes in mesh—
  even down to the leaning. They
      crouch now in the shade of a locust
  tree the arborist says
      is resistant to pollution and constraint—

or maybe just resistant to
    nothing in particular.

λ

Archangels, despite lofty titles, are actually lowest...
*   *nearest to earth and cities. We know them—*
dread trumpets of fire and plague.

Taxonomy in guise of hallowed choirs.

How do we defer to a heaven split?
*   *Even angels fall, shunted into categories. They*
ripple and yearn strong by stronger for proximity, light.

*   *Even on the blackest night of December*
*   *wretches stretched for the gaze of a father.*

Endemic filial jealousy—our common heritage
*   *rends sisters and stars alike into*
*   *endless sprawling.*

λ

Steel lines galvanize
    to shine earthward in rows, perforating light

round as the wheels that roll under them.
    every night, they
evolve colors, polychromatic by
    turns—sometimes blue, sometimes a shade
less appealing.

Insipid in its growing utility,
    gas burns, growing broad—
      hair on swayed backs. An aging horse

turns west, away from the gathering
    storm.

λ

Over the viaducts I found entry,
    forgotten now as the tracks they spanned.
Below them railroads, switchyards were
    lost under a crush of lofts and bars.

    Utility is temporal in such places,
        enduring only so long as
      money and industry hold out.

            Endings come here not in a whistle,
                rather a curtailed bleat
              caught in wind and throats of sheep.

        unhinged by the steepness of a chute,
              redolent of cinders that trains belched before
        youth and desire rendered all obsolete.

People had always gathered there,
      ordinary,
    in their hopes,

        so simple—a roof, a meal
            or just a boxcar out of the rain—
        nowhere better or darker left to go.

λ

Grist is what the city clamors for now.
    Everyone wants texture,
      original artifacts of a failed industrial past...

like scales and concrete and meat hooks. Look
    out through triple-pane UV glass.
    Grime out there is dipped in lucite

in a vain attempt at preservation—
    canning a city in dread of winter.

𝜆

Inspirational dioramas and Santa Claus heads
    nod in shops at Christmas.
    Fa la la la la deck the halls—we went to see them.

        In a storm with the avenues silent,
          light formed a nimbus around streetlamps,

        tickled by snow that sped up down alleys, then
          ranged wide in twirls at intersections.

At the corner of 18th and Broadway was a church,
    Trinity Methodist lit with tapers.

        In the parking lot I remember slush,
          on the sidewalk salt,
            nativity scene propped in the snow by heavy doors.

λ

Out on the edges the city of memory thins,

frays into purple threads.

λ

Debris lines the banks of Clear Creek.

    Everywhere I look are plastic sacks and paper cups,

limp skeletons of coffee and commerce

    infecting bunchgrass like packrat nests.

    Remember the day the creek foamed?

        It looked for all the world like a can of Coors

    upended until its story became a river,

my bare feet cringed when I waded into cold.

λ

Nighttime excursions in winter had more
    of the taste of fear to them,
creeping through derelict buildings
    to rooms littered with old forms.

λ

> Urban and urbane are separated by
> recklessness—
>
> nothing to do with sound,
>   and everything to do with
>
>   lying.

Unexpectedly, it all tastes like autumn now.
    Red sunsets and sunrises are the same product of spinning
brown in the sky,

    and so much depends on which way the city's facing:
      nearly east or hardly west by morning.

λ

Railroads started it all—

    answer on a history quiz—

next came mines with ghosts, candles, and
    tailings dripped cyanide downhill (with names like Argo and Climax and).

                      In the city immigrants came to spend
                            nights in clubs with people who understood
                    gambling, drinking, dreaming of home.

Flung dice rattled off the sooty wall and the youth
    leaned in a doorway, flapping sweaty bills in his hand.

Uneasy with money, he threw again and again,
        intent on losing most everything to avoid ending up
    dead. Or worse.

λ

Anything can happen in a city

spread so wide nobody can see from one gap to the next.

λ

Summers exist in memory as braided evenings,
    never just nights, but semi-dark.
      Outside—in latticed chairs we dragged circles.

    Warped pine in the mountains and
        fog of exhaust downtown
      lingered over the battered fence.

All the raggedy teenagers contained,
    keeping time over coffee,
      exchanging opinions about packed dirt, fire, and

              slipping. Secrets tongued earlobes.

Broken shadows and police arrived.
    Understandably,
    they knew how to hide from curfews—

      training one eye to the door at midnight,
        hearing menace in adult voices,
      ever so sinister to adolescent tones.

        Youthful innocence is something
          wistful as falling words on
        ears not yet ringing.

  Run.
    Everyone run for the alley. Stay clear of the light.

λ

Bright pink and blue hang on the night side of creation.

Eyes might track light's spread
    as they track the line of wind that
undulates through foxtail grass.

The prairie to the east swallowed the first
    immigrants into sod and fields; they
fell along contours of rivers.

Up exposed guts into discovered continents—
    lands waited for light from anywhere but above.

λ

Can my memory of beauty possibly
   have faded so much?

      Rampant cynicism seems to
          overrun my faith in alleys as playgrounds.
     My hands no longer warm over burning trash.

At least not with
   that tingle they used to have.

       Inside the abandoned brick factory,
          closed off from snow where kilns once baked,
      indefinite shadows danced on rust walls.

      Near the tracks where wagons dumped
        the last remains crumble—
     hand-formed clay in piles.

Even on nights smudged with clouds
   I could finger the bricks' tippy weight,
  rough edges in a jumbled rising.

Where were they meant for? Whose then
   ardent hands had hoped to build, lost
  youth to arthritis waiting for fresh blocks?

        In such hands what city might have sprung?

λ

Now clapboard
 trademarks and brown-paint-glazed
  houses crawl out of sawdust, glue.

Epoxy replaced mortar—needle injected
 slip joints extend beyond reason,

  track the veins of structures.

Arms crease with tourniquet bruises.
 Raised vessels sprawl, canopic.
  Sanguinely we erect addictions, just as quickly abandon them.

λ

The lights went up in car lots, then streets and parks.
    Hyundai dealerships lit like Casablanca;
  erotic veils danced far below a blue Atlantic horizon.

    Before long there were arc lamps
        running double-time on main drags.

    In stadiums, crowds
          gouge stars from a vast radius of sky,
     hurl a lint of blue.

Try to squint through; there is nothing
  except maybe the moon, or another

                searchlight gimbaled
                    to a helicopter, "police" on its side.

            Amazing how strong the instinct to run.
              No need to. We convince ourselves

all is for our protection.

Light brings vision. And knowledge is safety, they say.
    Ordinary incandescence failed so miserably—as
  gaslamps in parlours failed before.

λ

On this side of the mountains, everyday spring
   feels farther away.

Twisting at the end of winter's rope,
   how did her neck ever stretch so long?

Especially in the city's maze
   concrete canyons and wind,

inhumanity sinks chills no collar could fend,
   turned up to ears and higher.

Yellow paint ices white on slushy curbs—
    the view with our faces bent down.
   Edges sharpen.

                  Rubbed hands yield little.

                  Massaged ears still throb
                      inside black gloves,
                no stiff concern.

Altruistic cold levels things and all
   live homeless in days spent under a filthy sun.

λ

Misanthropy and duty
      overran good intentions.
    Random manifestations might lift the city now.

                Aromatic acrobats arrive in armfuls by trapeze.
                I see the red circus,
                    never before so grand, never so musical.

        Even peanut shells crumble like xylophones.

    Only this event will be advertised exclusively by billboard.

                    λ

    Cartilage crept to my lungs over night—a mortared torso.

        Or at least that's how it feels.

    No exhalations wheeze without
        fisted demand of a cough. I am rattled.

    Every time I pause between breaths, cracklings and pops
        slip out my throat as uncontrolled milk—
    sounds of cereal, cellophane.

                I think I've finally rounded into a cul-de-sac.
                    Once breathing was easy under nightlights;
              now it's difficult and darkness frightens me.

Fever dreams collapsed.

        Ashamed to even write.

    Really no point denying I'm deeply sick.

Crystalline aches have scraped into joints.

            Lucidity is a drip.

        And I can't even think clearly. Let alone put words down.

My language is sticky-thick like the white coating my
    palate, making it impossible to open up,
  swallow a lukewarm glass of water.

Spit in a toilet first thing in the morning.
   Pray to the god of clear breathing.
  Receive the only answer forthcoming,

        encoded in barks and coughs like
            an Olde English song of heroes
           dead from sword wounds to lungs.

I inhale gasps of phlegm, blood, pine smoke,
   now wind whistles under the eaves and my mug of cider lies empty.

λ

Snow begins falling in clumps on grass.

    Picture the bluebird there through my fever—

erect at the tip of the sequoia,
    clutching green needles in front of the red metal barn.

                      That is the kaleidoscope polis I
                            remember in all its playfulness.
                        Anyone could run their fingers through it,

                    linger on spinning colors passing by.

$$\lambda$$

Myopic is how I see light at night.

Elliptical cobwebs extend,
       rigid as plate glass, and
  incapable of compromise.

          Dark is dark, and light light.
            It is the shadows that know difference.

          And they only share secrets with the blind,
             never with nocturnal pedestrians
                stepping over puddles on the way to the store...

any store at all with cigarettes, or
   beer in suitcases, at a closeout price.
Oscillating red and blue lights strobe the parking lot,
   verify the peril of situations.

       Everyone is just holding on,
          and the fingernails are peeling back.

             New nerves hurt the worst.
            Dead ones, the least.

Between streetlight and convenience we
   evaluate the arithmetic flash.

Listing then in the crunch
    of broken bottles,
  we have nothing but to watch, and watch.

λ

Everyone in the city should ride the bus at least once.

Viscosity of a community is best measured by that stick—
    oil-soaked humanity steams in the heat,
  lubricated into seats by fear, and, sometimes,

underwhelming courtesy... where it's safe to nod but not
   touch. Never, never touch

      Instilled warnings about porcupines and panthers infect,
        only this time fellow people,
      nearby stewing in fiberglass.

Orange must be the color of surplus and cheapness.
   For what other reason pick it over blue?

        Scraped feet on rubber leave
          traces of gravel and sloppy salt.

Reach for a dangling handle if
   every bucket is taken.

     Etch that feeling in memory:
        the surface of the loop is the viscosity of the city.
     Luckily, in this case only four.

I wipe my hand against my jeans.
   Get a transfer.

        Heaving a backpack onto my shoulder I step into dark.
        That's how things end up—
      standing in the snow watching a dirty bus pull away.

λ

Black encrusts its backside,
        even encroaches on the poster proclaiming
    Come See the Paradise!

or,
    maybe, just *Listen to Kool Jazz at Work!*

        Everyone has to listen to something, I suppose.
            And even though fusion jazz gives me migraines,
        let's assume that somebody out there
            in this festering metropolis adores the stuff—

even would push over the receptionist by the coffee machine to get it.
    Never mind the ficus.

λ

Vivisection means nothing to such people.

And I literally mean nothing.

Plebeians become plutocrats while my back's turned.

Overgrown self-image is the norm. They get
reinforced, and reinforced again.
In this long game we're all winners, see?

Zoos are just parks, now, with taller fences.
Endearing, isn't it?

Don't even try to figure which side I'm on. From a
practical standpoint,
I promise judging this is a waste of time.

No pin has been fast enough yet to impale me on a musical donkey.
Kneecaps are my only real weakness, that and
sodium lamps, but I've mentioned those before.

As well as stale urban planning.

Latent strings in our guts
turn our heads in squares, around grids.

Blocks, we call them, despite unredeemable flatness.
Lamentable in their shallowness, they are
unstackable semantics.

Research by engineers must have been
    responsible, I think, must have been inextricable from
  encroachment of ninety-degree geometry into human spaces.

                Didn't we used to live in caves?
                      Play with our children in fields?
                And even bathe in streams?

    Never in life would I
        disrobe and dip into the
  effervescent churning rush of this
      metropolis' opaque rivers.

                It's hard to even consider them such; walled in
                    concrete twenty feet high on both sides.

        Oh sure, we might give them bike paths
              for company or maybe a tree for
          shade, just a spot between asphalt.

People doze under honey locusts,
    recline against the occasional scarred trunk.

Even I have sunk down
      after sprinklers have done their daily work
  dampening soil and green grass.

                In the night both are black equally,
                    no distinguishing between except by texture.

        Gone are greens and reds of sunshine,
            forgotten the tones revealed in full light.

λ

    Under the pink glow everything looks
      gruesome as a cadaver's calf

upended on a steel table. The scalpel
  extends as a blade of vertigo from drunks spinning in the park at night.

        Halfway is no way to talk about these things.
         Even I know I've been pulling punches.

   Retching and raving, I
     explore my throat with a dirty fingernail—
the crust of the city scraped away,

    handling railings and treetrunks, groping with my eyes closed.

       Embed the mingled DNA from millions,
        some of them human—
      tap dancers, performance artists,
       and buskers oh my.

Remind me again why the monkey got stuck cranking tunes?

    Seems to me that's where the real show was.

Forget the guy in the hat,
   it's the little fella we should keep our eyes on. Just
  nod in time with the crank.

Dented the box may be now, but
  no plinking ever sounded so synchronistically spontaneous as an
organ box wheezing its way,
  seizing at the base of each turn, same as

       I seize at the bottom of each breath,

     stopping before my lungs draw their next
      tacky pull of smog off idling cabs. I
     exhale dregs as fog in air.

Recirculating carbon we all share
  swirled with mud down storm drains.

        λ

Cottonwoods bloom in tinsel strings.

    Ochre like flakes of blood, I've
        never doubted their parts;
   their conjugal biology dangles in plain view.

            Awkward and fragile, at least
                in a spring storm,
           nascent leaves collect weight like the lonely
                elephant at the zoo collects fences after a rampage.

Dull rage at beatings
    that faded years ago—
  her pacing tamps ellipses into dirt.

Exemic skin greys under dust and straw,
    crinkles as she walks. She stares

into the blue eyes of children, bobbing
    toddlers behind pink cotton candy.

           Yet she plods with the mass of all of her accrued
              feminine dignity,
          intent on the young that climb and
              nudge against her stockade.

           Dignity, I think again, and
             stinking anger ooze from her
       nipples, her tattered ears—given the chance
          over the moat she'd leap,

  soaring skyward, growing tusks her sex never shared.

Kneeling, I'd wait for the crush.

You know, try to make peace with my maker before
     flattened by some righteously indignant pachyderm. One clearly with all
laws of nature and decency on her side.

𝜆

Am I losing focus?

The zoo is the city's, just like I am, just like the circus—
    constrained by chains forged red,
   elemental wristlets—iron and iron and iron.

      I wouldn't have the courage to stray from
        lights that haunt my days as well as nights.

      I see them whenever I press my palms against my eyes. I
        need an escape into blackness, but I'm too timid to
      gouge, or poke, or even bandage.

$$\lambda$$

Over there is exactly where the planks were.

Frames supported their red and their white stripes, a line of
      orange cones in the weeds,
   rubber in thistles rotting to rigidity.

And I'm sure that was where Broadway ended.
     Not because of signs,
   god no, but behind the barricade was dark.

$$\lambda$$

Every boy I knew adored collisions.

Running full tilt and sliding at each other
        over meticulously polished snow. WHUMP-
   toppled into a mess of combat boots and leather jackets.

Teenagers must have rubber
   in them, and hemlock,

nestled in joints where
       giggling starts, and
   gangrene, but only when broken.

                Lying sprawled now on my back,
                    age arrives with satchels in the shape of impacts.
              Snowflakes float across the screen of clouds.

              Snowflakes drift and collide with eyelashes.

$$\lambda$$

       Only, it's not as pretty as all that in my head.

    Prometheus had his rock. I have my city.
        And I conjure an eagle, he
      quietly swings my bile wide. I

unmake the reds and blues and greys. They cobbled such
    even, unbending lines.
      Take back Russian olives, pastures, silos—all milestones of escape.

          Amplify them to the vividness of ravens
            undulating in the wind:
              that hiss along the wire of childhood.

$$\lambda$$

Ossified benches tilt under stunted trees,
    looking so much like driftwood
  or the staved bones of an orphan

grey whale run aground in flight
    of loneliness or despair.
  Uncertainty.

                Street urchins and borrowed cigarettes—
                    my memories sank in concrete.
                Arcana

                scribbled on granite monoliths.

                They called this a park—
                  upended trash cans and
                red stains on brick—could have been
                    blood, ketchup, or...

                And these tattered kids pranced like royalty.

                Their flannel shirts dangled tuxedo tails,
                    oligarchy of homeless children
                regal with grim teeth,
                    yellow as an autumn sun.

  Gurgles ripple from manhole covers,
      ripple over streets in shrouds of steam.
    Opening curtains swallow Lincolns whole.

                Up near the rooftops

        nearer still to sky, ghosts of
            derelict pigeons circle,
        entranced by warmth. High.

Divorced, finally, from shadows in alleys below.

λ

I rode an elevator up 47 floors with my parents,
    nearly to the top of some bank tower. But I don't
remember the bronze sculpture or oily
    ephemera I saw there. I cannot forget

        clambering back down,
          every stair a terror to ground,

        needing descent, and solidity, driven
          timid by the
         drunken swaying of buildings in wind.

And my father fell with me,
    yelling, *let's race let's race!*

step by step by leap,
      and my mother dressed in black,
    nodded by the elevator.

                λ

Distant thunder grumbled off sandstone
    anticipation alum-dry, and
linty clouds of listless flannel
    loitered overhead.

                              But east were blackness and
                                    ugly purpling anvils,
                              towers of nimbus
                                      building to hailstorm.

Up above the city nestled in red music
    rocks and scrub oak

I was with friends—and yet
    envying the storm, the
  driving ruin, the battering.

                                        λ

I watched with delight as the limeade can popped into the air.
    Nearing its apex it tipped,
  sliding at back to ground.

    My father twisted the fuses of two firecrackers together,
        only trusting himself with a task so delicate. But I
    knew I would touch a match to sputtering.

I would be the one to run—fear
    nipping at hands splayed over ears.

        Glory! Bang-shot
            can skyward again ten whole feet at least.

    On the grass a tongue of smoke licked
        blue stink of cordite.

    Blotchy soot clung around its mouth,
        lips, the sterile kiss of fire.

Eventually we ended with snakes,
  probably because all else was gone.

Reaching into the sack and
    eyeing that last box, mournfully
  digging through sawdust for a black pellet.

    Engulfed in blue flame they sizzled, smoked, and swelled.
        Tangling back on themselves, they glowed orange then faded.
    Embers—

Remember—

$$\lambda$$

Mistletoe with plastic berries and a red ribbon
      in a cellophane pouch,
    nativity scenes set out on cardboard with green felt, and

excelsior—my mother
      didn't have to drag me
    right past the glass and tinsel,

especially didn't need to show me all the lights we'd never have, but

                      she did, and
                            I stared at them as I skidded past.
                    Green, and red, and gold, and blue twinkled.

        No, I
                tried to explain, I just wanted lights at night—
          one string for the tree.

    She said our tree was old-fashioned,
        and, if anything, it would have candles. But since candles were
  fire hazards on a Douglas fir, we had none.

Eleven years later I propped an electric candelabra in my bedroom window.

λ

This I believe with all my still
   young illusions and faith:

the yellow plug I cast in the pond
   had no chance of catching anything.

It was only practice—
   solid rubber, no hooks

protruding or snagging, just for tossing past
   unsuspecting fish. My father was wary of
risks hidden in points—stories involving pierced

   ears and fingers.

   Did he think I didn't know,

   I wouldn't smell the lie in
     stunted projects, the
   guaranteed futility

of it all?

Rather, I think he intended it.
   Goading me all the way, I
ended up pissed off, spitting in water.

   Did I say I believe?

Say instead I'm sure.
   On June mornings my father
didn't care if I caught a fish or not.

   I did.

λ

Under my sleep I breathe a
    mumbled mantra:

              I believe in the tiptoeing heron,
                    thin legs of willow sticks,
                knobbly knees and all.

              I believe in the creosote that drips
                  liquid-sticky in the sun. Oh,

              let me believe, too, in the
                    stumbling, the shuffling people
                on the sidewalks, in this

              night, in this city.

              Let me believe in all the colors I imagine—
                  yellow, green, black, grey, red, pink, and blue.

These colors I have seen,
    how they glowed and bled,
    enveloped me.

Haloes slid from top to bottom in the rear window,
    entering me as I lay back
    and fell asleep on the vinyl seat of my parents' car.

λ

Rickshaws and straw hats invoke exotic places.

    This frontier burg I wrote barely boasts taxis.

        And god help you if you should
            need a ride on New Year's Eve.

Dented yellow they are unreachable—
    tissue-fragile with frost and
hidden, always hidden in the middle lanes.

λ

Except for my thin grandfather
 no one dies in my city.

Once was enough and
 now I forbid it.

Let them all live on forever.

Young, old.
  Sly or kind.
 Let them stay.

λ

Once I reached out my hand and caressed a lamp post

    wet from the rain,

loving the feel of alloy under my fingertips,

    yearning for a white figure to appear and show it was okay to cross.

λ

Under the Sky They Lit Cities

and there were streetlights
of blue mercury poison.
geologic infiltration of delirium
nocturnal urban ranting, fluid as snowflakes.
but they were beautiful
chromatic in their way, in the stars
the brightest, analog of the city.
terminal moraine of arc lamps
spread in spectral meridians above and below.

evolution of streetlights
become alien vaporized pink salt,
blurred pandemic of spreading fugue.
here, the stars find no sisters.
contained, the city finds no sky.
flat ceiling of orange rotting glass:
opaque, tautologous, masturbatory,
grounded in recent days and all but buried
in smoking cobble pre-determined.
resign to safety this pure disgorged sodium—
it kills only the heart,
and then
only slowly.

Whiteout, Early Morning

black ice under the Highway 7 overpass
when the Lincoln Continental broke loose
in front of me,
began its
slow orbital.
steel.
fractals   crossing lanes.

no   braking,
no turning.
just straight body clench, *I*
hope
it's gone before.

no prosaic string
of life,
strobes, wife,
home kids dog only
oh shit.

disappeared,
with a puff
in a snowbank.

Travis Cebula lives, writes, edits, and teaches in Golden, Colorado with his beautiful wife, Shannon. His poetry, photography, essays, and short stories have appeared internationally in both print and online journals. He is the author of four chapbooks. *Under the Sky They Lit Cities* is his first full-length collection of poetry.

Made in the USA
Charleston, SC
10 November 2010